Sumi-e

Sumi-e

The Art of
Japanese
Brush Painting

Shingo Syoko

CHRONICLE BOOKS

SAN FRANCISCO

First Published in the United States
in 2002 by Chronicle Books

Text © 2002 The Ivy Press Limited

Paintings © 2002 Shingo Syoko

This book was conceived, designed,
and produced by

THE IVY PRESS LIMITED
The Old Candlemakers, West Street
Lewes, East Sussex BN7 2NZ

Creative Director: Peter Bridgewater
Publisher: Sophie Collins
Editorial Director: Steve Luck
Design Manager: Tony Seddon
Designer: Andrew Milne
Senior Project Editor: Caroline Earle
Photographer: Ian Parsons
Additional Illustrations: Coral Mula
Picture Researcher: Vanessa Fletcher

ISBN-10 0-8118-3438-7
ISBN-13 978-0-8118-3438-4

Distributed in Canada by
Raincoast Books
9050 Shaughnessy Street
Vancouver, B.C. V6P 6E5

10 9 8 7 6 5

Chronicle Books LLC
85 Second Street
San Francisco, CA 94105
www.chroniclebooks.com

Contents

PART ONE

The Story of Sumi-e

In Japanese, *sumi* means "ink"; *sumi-e*, therefore, is the art of drawing with ink. Like so many of the fine arts of Japan, it was introduced from China, where examples have been found that are nearly four thousand years old. To the ancient Chinese, sumi-e was the perfect expression of Taoist beliefs—the circle in which we all live, the path leading through life. These ideas were passed on when sumi-e came to Japan, and it became an accepted principle that a few simple brushstrokes could express everything in the world, from the earth to the sky, and all the living creatures in it.

Around 700CE, the first examples of sumi-e began to emerge in Japanese art, displaying the crisp, linear style derived from China. By the Heian period (794–1185CE), sumi-e had developed into a refined art, practiced by scholars and monks and by the ladies and gentlemen of the Heian emperor's court. Both calligraphy and painting used brushes, and the speed and fluidity of the dancing strokes of calligraphy became incorporated into ink drawings. Indeed, it was usual to combine drawing and calligraphy on a single scroll or sheet of paper; just as a *haiku* is a poem expressing a thought in just three lines, so the drawings that accompany them suggest an idea with just a few strokes of the brush.

During the early part of the seventeenth century, Japan closed its borders to the outside world, and a uniquely Japanese style in brush drawing emerged— simple, serene, and breathtaking in its economy and elegance of expression. With the opening of the country's gates to the outside world in 1854, Japan experienced an enormous influx of foreign culture, and the impact of European art meant that traditional Japanese arts, including sumi-e, were to be almost forgotten until

Tenshin Okakura, a Japanese scholar of humanities, and Ernest F. Fenollosa, an American philosopher, reevaluated sumi-e for its exquisitely artistic qualities and eagerly introduced it to foreign countries. Today, sumi-e has acquired a variety of styles that reflects the diversity of the artistic tastes of the modern world.

Art and thought

The ancient art of brush painting is strikingly beautiful in its simplicity. Elegant, restrained, and serene, it expresses all of nature's beauty in tones of black ink on white paper. An ancient Chinese saying states, "When you have ink, you have color." In other words, the myriad colors in nature can be conveyed through nuances of tone, from rich, velvety black to a whisper of gray.

Sumi-e is not merely a decorative art, however. Technique is only part of the equation, and the artist is not merely concerned with making a literal representation of his subject. Spirituality has much greater importance, and the artist must get to the inner essence of the subject and translate his impression of it onto paper, simply and naturally, using the subtle tonal qualities of ink alone.

This attitude has its roots in three philosophies: Taoism, Buddhism, and Confucianism. A basic tenet of Taoism is the belief that the forces of nature—Yin and Yang—oppose and equalize each other, so there is always balance and unity. This concept underlies the principles of brushwork and composition in all Chinese and Japanese painting. Empty space, for example, is used as a positive compositional element, balancing the shapes made by the brush. Taoism and Zen Buddhism also stress the virtue of simplicity—hence the use of simple subjects such as flowers, birds, and trees—and economical brushstrokes

in black ink alone. Zen is an important element in sumi-e; the ritualized steps in learning the art impart a calming effect on the artist and the spectator.

Confucius stressed the importance of high moral standards and sincerity of thought and action. Thus, a sumi-e painting that shows spontaneity and feeling, even if it is a little awkward in execution, is held in greater esteem than one that is technically accomplished but lacking in feeling.

The basic strokes used in sumi-e are all found in the techniques for painting the four plants known as "the Four Gentlemen." These are the bamboo, the wild orchid, the chrysanthemum, and the plum tree. Each of these plants has an individual identity and meaning in Chinese culture, and each requires a different set of brushstrokes to depict its character correctly; it was said that if you could paint all of the four "gentlemen," you were well on your way to becoming a true artist.

Previous page: During the eighteenth century, a distinctively Japanese form of Chinese painting emerged, known as Nanga. *An example of this is* Night, *by Buson Yosa.*

Left: Fukurojin, the God of Longevity by Jakuchu Ito, c. 1790. During the late Edo period (1603–1868), among the various schools of sumi-e, arose artists such as Jakuchu Ito, who became known for an eccentric, vigorous style.

Above and opposite:
Waka-shikishi (Poem
Cards) *by Sotatsu
Tawaraya. Active during
the early part of the
seventeenth century,*

*Sotatsu Tawaraya was
a very ambitious artist
and created a totally
new style of expression
with decorative yet
dynamic images.*

The sets of brushstrokes that you need to learn are laid out in Part Four of this book. This introduces you to each of the Four Gentlemen and takes you through the strokes needed to paint each one, in a logical and time-honored sequence. Once you have mastered the basic skills and can execute combinations of strokes, later chapters offer new applications for them, from fish and birds to figures and landscapes.

Remember, sumi-e is as individual as handwriting, and it may take a little time to develop your personal style. Don't get too discouraged if your early attempts are unsuccessful; even the great masters of ink painting had to practice their strokes every day! Be patient. With regular practice the brush movements will become second nature; the *chi* (energy) will flow from your mind to your hand and you will draw with the sureness of touch and depth of feeling that are the hallmarks of sumi-e painting.

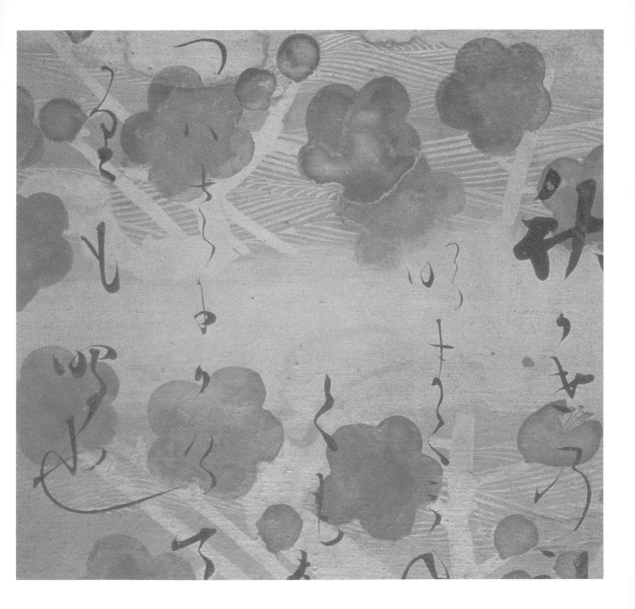

PART TWO

The Four Treasures

The influence of calligraphy permeates all of Japanese art, and the basic tools used by sumi-e painters are the same as those used by calligraphers. Writing materials have been held in high esteem in Oriental culture for over two millennia, since Confucius deemed literary accomplishment to be one of the primary virtues. Especially prized are the ink stick (*sumi*), the inkstone (*suzuri*), the brush (*fude*), and the paper (*kami*). These are known as the Four Treasures of the Scholar's Studio.

The ink (*sumi*)

Ink for sumi-e comes in the form of a solid rectangular stick. The best ink is made from pine soot and animal glue, which produces a brilliant, glossy ink with a brown-black tone. Pine wood is burned in a kiln, and the soot from the smoke is scraped off the kiln walls, mixed with glue, perfumed with sandalwood, then pressed into molds and left to harden.

Another method uses the soot collected from the smoke of burning oil, and this ink has a blue-black tone. Experts can distinguish which type of soot has been used in the making of a specific ink stick and will study the tone and hue of the ink to assess a stick's quality.

Antique sumi are often elaborately decorated with relief landscapes, animals, or birds and inlaid with gold and are regarded as art forms in themselves. Rare and precious sumi, from a particular dynasty or maker, are highly prized by scholars and connoisseurs of art.

Opposite: The brush (fude) used in sumi-e is made of layers of animal hair, such as sheep, horse, deer, and raccoon dog (tanuki) hair, which makes it very absorbent.

The inkstone (*suzuri*)

To produce liquid ink for painting, the ink stick is ground with water on an inkstone, or suzuri. Antique suzuri, like sumi, are highly prized by collectors for their artistry. They are made from hard materials such as copper, iron, jade, and quartz, often formed into exquisite shapes such as lily pads and flowers.

Modern-day suzuri are made from smooth ceramic, nonporous slate, and either natural or artificial stone. Chinese Duanxi stone is especially popular because of its beautiful black color and the mysterious patterns that are sometimes seen in its surface. Suzuri are mostly rectangular in shape and have a flat surface that slopes down to a shallow well at one end, in which the liquefied ink is held. Inkstones come in many sizes: some are huge and can be up to 3 feet (1 meter) long; others are the size of a matchbox.

CARE OF THE SUMI

A sumi stick should be handled with care because it is liable to break if dropped. It is also vulnerable to dampness and humidity. After painting, dry the sumi stick with a soft cloth to prevent it from cracking, and store it in a box. Throw away any ink remaining in the well of the suzuri (it should not be reused) and wipe away all traces of dried ink on the grinding surface.

The brush (*fude*)

Oriental paint brushes are made from sheep's wool and the hair of horses, goats, rabbits, squirrels, and so on. Good quality bristles are selected, sorted into even lengths, and combed to remove any weak ones. The hairs are cut into five different lengths and shaped into a cone, with the sturdier bristles on the outside, and then bound and glued into a hollow bamboo handle. This construction makes the brush strong, flexible, and versatile in use. The thick, tapering head can make broad strokes and can be drawn up to a very fine point for painting delicate lines.

There are special brushes for drawing very thin lines, thick lines, and so on, but the one most often used in sumi-e is an all-purpose brush called the *tsuketate*. It has firm, durable bristles made from sheep wool mixed with horse or deer hair and with raccoon dog (*tanuki*) hair at the tip.

CARE OF THE BRUSH

When you buy a new brush, remove its protective plastic cover and don't put it on again because it will damage the bristles. The bristles are stiffened with size to retain the finely pointed shape; remove this by soaking for a few minutes in cool water.

After use, rinse the brush well, dry it on a soft cloth, then smooth the tip between your finger and thumb. Leave the brush to dry horizontally or hang it up, pointing downward (some brushes have a loop at the end of the handle for this purpose). Once dry, store your brushes in a box or rolled up in a bamboo place mat.

The paper (*kami*)

The first true paper is reputed to have been invented in China in 105CE, from matted vegetable fibers. Today there is a huge variety of Chinese and Japanese papers available, made from materials such as mulberry bark, hemp, bamboo, and rice straw. The qualities of these papers—thickness, absorption, texture—vary widely, influencing the effects of ink and brush. Therefore, it is crucial to choose the right kind of paper to achieve the results you desire. When painting in the *mokkotsu* style, for instance, in broad strokes, an absorbent paper works better than a sized paper. In this sense, it is safe to say that paper holds a place of paramount importance in the art of sumi-e.

Among the many kinds of Chinese paper, *xuanzhi*, produced in Xuanzhou of Anhui Province, has always been the most popular paper with calligraphers and sumi-e painters, Chinese and Japanese alike. This paper contains a percentage of rice straw, which gives it excellent absorbency and allows expression of subtle tones of ink. However, the inclusion of straw also means that the paper is relatively fragile, and therefore sumi-e painters sometimes prefer to use single- or double-backed xuanzhi for its strength.

In Japan, handmade paper (*washi*) is still being produced using bast fibers from the paper mulberry (*kozo*), *mitsumata*, and *gampi* plants. Traditional Japanese papermaking is enormously labor-intensive. Unlike Western paper, which has short fibers, traditional washi has long fibers and thus has great strength and durability. Machine-made papers emulating washi are also popular. *Gasenshi* paper is the favorite choice for practice work because it is inexpensive and absorbs the sumi easily and well.

Although sumi-e painters don't normally work on Western paper, it can be fun to experiment with good-quality watercolor papers in addition to the paper in the pack. Cartridge paper is not suitable because it is too heavily sized.

Opposite: The textures of paper that can be used for sumi-e vary widely and will influence the final effect of your painting.

ACCESSORIES

This pack contains the Four Treasures —all the materials you need to start learning to paint with a brush. As your skill increases, you may want to add the following items.

- Although different tones of gray can be mixed in the well of the inkstone, this takes some skill and you may find it easier to use a small shallow dish of white ceramic for mixing dark ink with water to obtain gray washes. You can also control the amount of water in your brush by pressing it against the rim of the dish.

- You may also find a *hissen* useful; this is a ceramic container divided into three sections, used for rinsing out brushes.

- To store your brushes safely, roll them up in a small bamboo mat, or *fudemaki*.

- It is important that your paper is held firm and steady while you are working, so place a paperweight or other heavy object along the top of the paper.

- It is advisable to place a piece of felt or other soft cloth under the paper to prevent ink from staining your work surface.

PART THREE

Getting Ready for Practice

If you are new to the art of sumi-e, you will need to learn how to prepare your tools—and yourself—for painting. In this chapter you will learn the "mechanics" of how to grind the sumi and how to load and handle the brush correctly. In Oriental art, the process of getting ready to paint is an important, and enjoyable, part of the experience. Before you begin, make sure that you are in a calm frame of mind and that your working environment is quiet and free of clutter.

Right: Your posture influences your brush-strokes; be careful to keep your back straight but not too tense.

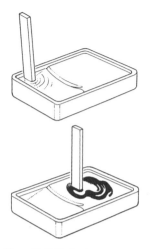

Above: Half fill the depression in the inkstone and dip the sumi stick in the water. Grind the stick vertically on the inkstone to achieve the depth of black desired.

Grinding the ink

To prepare ink for painting, place some water in the well of the suzuri—it should be about half full.

Dip one end of the sumi stick into the water, then place it vertically on the flat surface of the suzuri and begin rubbing with circular movements, slowly and with easy pressure. As the ink is ground, it runs down the sloping surface and mingles with the water in the well. Remoisten the stick when it begins to feel dry and sticky; this indicates that the water has absorbed all the ink it can.

Continue grinding, slowly and gently, for two or three minutes. This quiet and repetitive action has a calming effect, helping to clear the mind in preparation for the painting you are about to do. As the ink is ground, the sandalwood perfume is released, adding to the pleasure of the process.

To test the strength of the ink, dip a brush into it. The bristles should be a rich black; if they are gray, you need to grind more ink. Be sure to mix plenty of ink—the flow of your painting will be interrupted if you have to stop to grind more. Gray tones are achieved by pouring a little black ink from the suzuri into a shallow white dish or saucer and diluting to the desired shade with water. In this way you can have various tones of ink ready before starting to practice.

When you have finished grinding, prop the sumi on the edge of the suzuri so it is at hand if you need more ink. Never leave the wet sumi stick lying on the suzuri because the moistened glue in it will cause adhesion.

How to hold the brush

In sumi-e painting, a brushstroke can create a line as fine as the vein of a leaf or as rugged as a plum branch. But in order to achieve these effects you must first learn how to hold the brush correctly. The technique is quite different from that used in Western painting, but once you have mastered it, you will find it pleasant and relaxing.

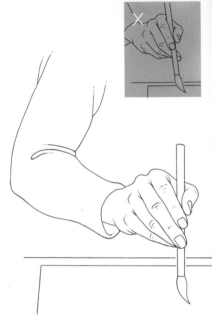

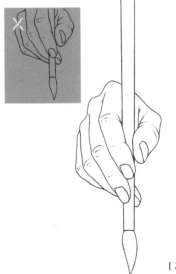

Hold the brush upright, quite high up on the shaft. Grip the shaft lightly between your thumb and index finger. Place the middle finger just below the index finger, then place the ring finger under the shaft to support it. No finger should touch the palm. The brush should be loosely held, not tightly gripped. This way you will be able draw both straight and curved lines without losing control.

Posture is important. Before beginning your practice, your back should be straight but not too tense, and your arms relaxed and free. Your hand, wrist, arm, and shoulder should move as a single unit, held clear of the paper, so that the energy, or *chi*, can flow freely from your mind to the brush.

Above: The brush should be held upright and tight enough to draw, but do not grasp it too firmly or hold it at a slant, because this will make lines weak and clumsy (see inset).

Left: Hold the brush lightly between the thumb and index finger with the middle finger below. The ring finger supports the brush shaft. Do not hold it as you would a pen with just thumb and index finger (see inset).

Sumi-e: The Art of Japanese Brush Painting

Above: Squeeze the washed brush across the edge of the hissen.

First, dip the brush in clean water and gently wipe off the excess on the side of the dish. The brush should be wet but not dripping. Hold the brush and dip the tip into the sumi; ink is absorbed from the tip of the brush, so it is thickest at the tip and weakest at the root.

Loading the brush

The Oriental paint brush is capable of an enormous variety of strokes and nuances of tone, depending on the amount of ink in the brush and the angle at which it is held.

Sumi-e strokes must be fluid but controlled. If there is too much water in the brush, control is lost and there is a danger of creating a *nijimi* effect—a halo of water appears around the stroke, spoiling its crisp appearance. If there is too little water in the brush, fluidity is lost and your painting will be dry and lifeless. With practice you will acquire a feel for the water-holding capacity of your brush.

Above: Dip only the tip of the brush in the ink.

Left: The ink is absorbed from the tip upward.

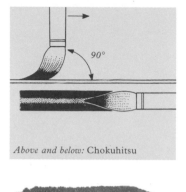

Above and below: Chokuhitsu

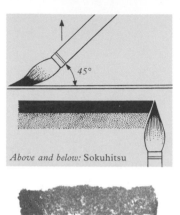

Above and below: Sokuhitsu

Above: Experiment with tones of ink. How much ink your brush absorbs will have different effects on the lines you draw.

Practice strokes

There are two basic strokes in sumi-e. With *chokuhitsu*, the brush is held vertically and the line drawn with the tip, keeping the wrist straight. This produces a thin, even stroke. With *sokuhitsu*, the brush is slanted at an oblique angle and the line drawn using the side of the bristles. This produces a broad stroke with one sharp edge and one soft edge.

Practice both of these techniques by drawing lots of different strokes: curved and straight, vertical, horizontal, thick and thin, dark and light. Draw freely and rhythmically.

Relax, enjoy moving your wrist, arm, and hand as a unit, and you will produce wonderful lines. The more you practice, the more control you will achieve with your brush.

Try varying the speed of the brush and the pressure applied and observe how this alters the depth of tone and also the character and feeling of the stroke. When the brush begins to run out of ink, it makes broken, dry brush strokes that are also expressive and complement the "wet" strokes. It is this combination of wet and dry, dark and light, slow and fast that gives life and vitality to a painting and expresses the spirit of the artist.

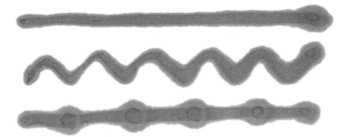

Above: Variations—try vertical and horizontal lines; and slanted, thicker, thinner, darker, and lighter lines. Also try drawing very slowly and very quickly.

Above: Experiment loading your brush to create light and dark shades.

Light and dark tones (*bokashi*)

The thick head of the brush can hold a lot of liquid, and it is possible to load it with light and dark color tones of ink at the same time. This lets you define, say, the light and shade on a bamboo stalk with a single brushstroke, thus achieving spontaneity and harmony. This shading technique is known as *bokashi*.

Dip the brush in water and wipe off the excess on the side of the dish. Then touch the tip to the black ink on the flat surface of the suzuri and then wait for the ink to be absorbed up the bristles. Touch the tip of the brush to the ink again to redarken the tip. The brush will now contain a gradation of three tones—dark at the tip, gray in the middle, and light at the base.

Now practice making bokashi strokes. When you hold the brush at an oblique angle, all three tones are used, because the whole body of the brush is in contact with the paper. By lifting the root of the brush you get two tones—dark and medium. Lift it farther, and only the tip is in contact with the paper, so you get a single, dark tone. You will be amazed by the variety and beauty of the ink tones you can produce by manipulating the brush. Also, different effects are achieved depending on whether the brush is wet or "thirsty," and on the type of paper you use.

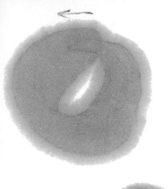

Drawing circles and dots

Pretend to be a child playing with a brush, drawing circles over and over. This is useful practice, especially for drawing flower petals. Again, vary the angle, the speed, and the pressure of the brush, and the amount of ink used. Your circles may be a bit irregular at first, but once you experience your mind connecting with the brush, you will quickly improve.

Painted dots are useful for creating natural patterns and textures in the landscape. Dots can be made by controlling the amount of ink the brush absorbs. Place the tip of the brush on the paper without hesitation, pause, then lift it quickly. The size and character of the dot—whether sharp or soft—depends on the wetness of the brush, how much pressure you apply and for how long, and the angle of the brush.

Above: To create a variety of dots, vary the amount of ink absorbed.

PART FOUR

The Four Gentlemen

(*Shi Kunshi*)

In the late seventeenth century a Chinese book, *The Mustard Seed Garden Manual of Painting* (1701), was introduced to Japan. It was a comprehensive course in painting, and beginners were advised to start the course by drawing four subjects— bamboo, plum, orchid, and chrysanthemum—because all the basic sumi-e brushstrokes are involved in painting these subjects. Besides providing excellent models for technical practice, these four plants hold an exalted place in Oriental culture, embodying qualities such as dignity, grace, strength, and nobility. They are known collectively as The Four Gentlemen (*Shi Kunshi*).

This section introduces you to each of the Four Gentlemen and examines the strokes you will need to render each in the traditional way. Each one is described precisely, in the form of an exercise. At first you will find it difficult to hold your brush in the prescribed fashion, and the strokes you make will be clumsy. But if you keep your arm relaxed and simply concentrate on completing each stroke without worrying about the next one, you will gradually find that the transitions between light and firm pressure and the different sweeps of the brush come more smoothly and naturally, and you will start to be able to express your own line.

In Japan, artists who have been working on sumi-e for many years will still sometimes use the strokes of the Four Gentlemen as warm-up exercises, much as musicians will practice scales. They are the basics and the building blocks of your style, and they are worth learning well.

KEY TO SYMBOLS

These symbols show you at a glance which brushstroke and which size brush to use.

 Small-sized brush

Medium-sized brush

Large brush

Chokuhitsu

Sokuhitsu

LESSON ONE

Bamboo

The bamboo is the quintessential symbol of Oriental art. This noble and graceful plant displays strength, vitality, and resilience. It bends beneath heavy weights of snow and does not break but springs back; thus it symbolizes the spirit to endure in adversity and the unyielding integrity of a gentleman of strong moral fiber.

The sumi-e painter is expected not only to depict the bamboo's physical shape but also to express its inherent spirit of resilience and strength. Try to visualize the whole plant before you start to draw—the stem shoots out from the ground, strong yet pliable. The graceful leaves catch even the tiniest breeze, making a soft, soothing sound. Make swift, firm, agile strokes using the whole brush, and try to complete your drawing "in one breath."

There are many varieties of bamboo, but the most common one is *tanchiku,* and this is the one you will learn to draw in this section.

The different parts of the bamboo —stem, branches, and leaves— involve interesting combinations of straight and curved lines, and you will also discover the expressive qualities of light and dark tone that give life and movement to the bamboo.

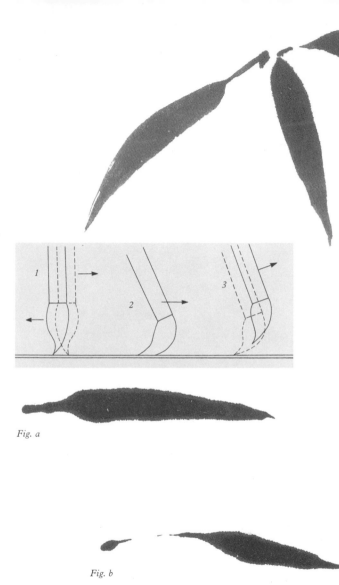

BASIC BRUSHSTROKES
Bamboo leaves

a] Bamboo leaves are broad and flat and taper to a point at each end. Load a medium-sized brush with black ink and wipe off the excess. For leaves in frontal view, hold the brush vertically and place the tip on the paper. Push it forward a little way, then pull it backward to draw the stalk *(Fig. a, 1)*. As the leaf broadens, hold the brush in chokuhitsu mode and apply pressure to broaden the stroke *(Fig. a, 2)*. As you reach the tip of the leaf, release the pressure and smoothly slide the brush from the paper and into the air *(Fig a, 3)*.

b] To draw a leaf in side view, use the chokuhitsu technique but lean the brush slightly. Draw each leaf with speed "in one breath" (in one stroke)—*Fig. b*.

Fig. a

Fig. b

c] Practice drawing leaves in groups of three to five *(Fig. c)*. Draw the whole group without redipping the brush, so that you get a variety of tones. Also vary the length and direction of the leaves and the speed of your strokes, to give life and vitality to the bamboo.

Fig. c

Fig. d

d] To depict leaves swaying in the wind *(Fig. d)*, use the tip of the brush to outline their shapes with thin, sharp lines (a technique called *koroku-ho*). Then fill in the shapes with ink. If you draw two sets of leaves in thick ink, then add another in the background in koroku-ho, you get a feeling of the wind blowing over them.

Bamboo stems

Use a large brush. To depict the rounded form of the stem with shading, ink up the brush with the bokashi method (*see page 24*). The main point to bear in mind when drawing bamboo stems is definitely speed. You must not hurry, but a line should be drawn in one move, using the whole brush from its tip to the root.

Each stem section is divided by a small gap to indicate the stem joint, but each stem should be painted with the idea of one continuous stroke. The stem sections are longer farther away from the ground but become shorter again near the top.

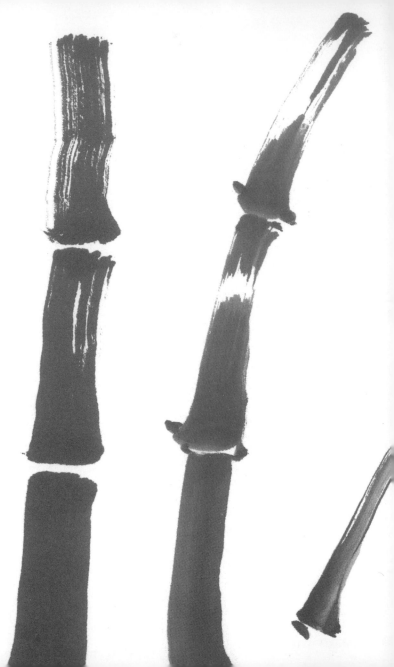

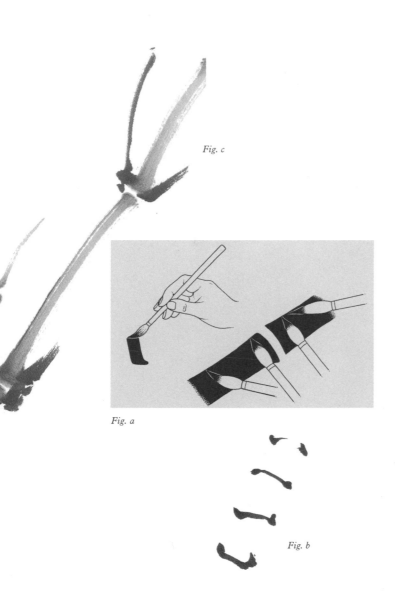

Fig. c

Fig. a

Fig. b

a] Using the sokuhitsu technique, lean the brush at a 45° angle so that the tip and side are in contact with the paper. Start at the bottom and draw the stem segments by pushing the brush upward, quickly and with even pressure. Leave a small gap after each section to indicate the joints *(Fig. a)*. Pause briefly at the beginning and end of each stroke; the ink will spread slightly to form the prominent ridges around the joints.

b] While the stems are damp, paint the knots that connect the sections with short horizontal strokes of dark ink using the brush tip *(Fig. b)*. Pause briefly at the beginning and end of the stroke and make it slightly curved to echo the roundness of the stalk.

c] Depict the slighter stems in sokuhitsu with a smaller brush. The joints are comparatively thicker and the stems between them very fine.

Bamboo branches

a] Dip a medium-sized brush into thick ink and blot it on scrap paper to remove the excess. Holding the brush vertically in chokuhitsu, draw lines upward. Draw with a quick, light, rhythmical movement to give life to the branches *(Fig. a)*.

Fig. a

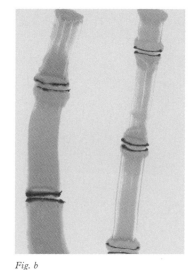

Fig. a

Fig. b

Combining the elements

Once you have mastered leaves, stems, and branches, you can put them all together to depict a complete bamboo plant and create your first work of sumi-e. As you draw, keep the enduring resilience and strength of the bamboo in mind and use swift, fluent brushstrokes.

a] Start with the stems because these form the basis of the composition *(Fig. a)*. Make light and dark tones to give variety and suggest the spatial relationship between the stems. A drier brush will leave stronger striations on the stem, adding to the poetry of the drawing.

b] Wait until the joint stems are a little dry but still damp, then draw the joint lines with thick ink *(Fig. b)*.

c] Next draw the branches with sharp, but fluid, lines *(Fig. c)*.

d] Draw each leaf group with a single brushload of ink. Try to capture the lithe grace of the leaves as they sway in the breeze *(Fig. d)*.

Fig. c

Fig. d

The Plum

What is customarily called a plum in Oriental painting is in fact a variety of apricot. The plum endures winter's cold and is the first tree to open its lovely blossoms in the still chilly air. Blooming soon after the New Year, it is a symbol of hope and rejuvenation. A popular image in sumi-e, and part of the set repertoire of bird-and-flower pictures, is that of a bush warbler on a plum branch; during the long winter months, this charming duo acts as a welcome reminder of the coming spring.

The plum is also admired for the interesting shapes of its twisted trunk and branches and the sweet fragrance of its blossoms. The Chinese associate the plum tree with a gentleman of grace, modesty, and perseverance.

In contrast to the simple, straight lines of the bamboo, the execution of the plum tree is more complex. In this lesson you will learn several skills that are needed for every aspect of brush painting. For example, you will learn how to combine wet and dry strokes to suggest the gnarled and rugged forms of the branches. In drawing the plum blossom you will be using curved lines and also the "boneless" method of drawing soft petals with no outlines.

Fig. b

c] Pink blossoms are drawn with no outline, using direct strokes. Dip your brush in light ink and wipe off the excess. Holding the brush upright, press the tip on the paper and press down while rolling the brush slightly. This makes a soft, round shape. Work quickly, otherwise the ink will spread too much and the petals will lose their shape *(Fig. c)*.

d] Use the tip of the brush to draw the stamens with dark ink. Make quick, flicking strokes, lifting the brush off the paper so that they taper to a point. Then add tiny dots at the ends of the stamens *(Fig. c)*.

BASIC BRUSHSTROKES
Plum blossoms

Each plum petal has a softly rounded shape, and five petals form a blossom.

a] White blossoms are expressed by outlines. Dip a small brush into gray ink and wipe off any surplus, keeping the point of the brush intact. Draw slightly elliptical circles, moving the whole brush and keeping it upright. Join the circles together to make a blossom *(Fig. a)*.

b] Draw plump circles to represent buds. One circle with two small ovals represents a side view of a half–opened blossom *(Fig. a and Fig. b)*.

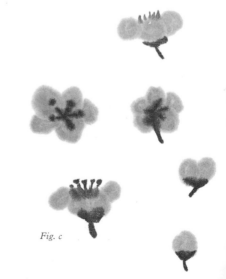

Fig. c

Fig. a

Fig. a

BASIC BRUSHSTROKES
Plum tree trunk

The trunk of the plum tree is gnarled and has sharp angles. Draw from the shoulder—if you draw from the wrist, the lines will be shaky and weak and not expressive of the vitality of a plum tree trunk.

a] Load a large brush with medium-gray ink. Angle the brush, bend the bristles, and draw a thick line upward in sokuhitsu with a slight force, following the angles of the trunk. Vary the pressure, allowing the contrasts of light and dark, wet and dry ink to suggest the rough bark. Then dot in some dark points representing moss *(Fig. a)*.

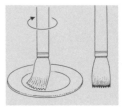

Fig. b, 2

b] Experiment with expressive textural marks. Here, the *kappitsu* (dry brush) technique suggests rough, dry bark *(Fig. b, 1)*. To achieve these broken strokes, blot the brush to remove excess water, then spread the bristles by pressing them on a saucer *(Fig. b, 2)* before dipping the brush in the ink.

c] For an advanced attempt, make use of various brush techniques, such as nijimi (soft, blurred effect), kappitsu, and *haboku-ho*. The haboku-ho technique is as follows: draw a line in weak ink, then add a touch of darker ink while the first stroke is still damp *(Fig. c)*.

Fig. b, 1

Fig. c

Fig. d

![icon]

BASIC BRUSHSTROKES
Plum tree branches

a] Use a medium-sized brush. Draw the branches and twigs quickly and lightly, with a free arm movement. Keep your brush lively and vary the pressure to bring texture, movement, light, and shade to the branches. Paint each branch "in one breath," without taking the brush off the paper. Stress the sharp angles natural to the plum tree *(Fig. d)*.

b] Make the joints by pausing slightly, and the thicker parts by pressing down with the brush. At the end of a branch, stop the stroke abruptly and lift the brush cleanly off the paper *(Fig. d)*.

c] For the finer twigs, pull the brush into the air to make a tapered point *(Fig. d)*. You can also use a drier brush for a lighter, more delicate effect.

Fig. a

Combining the elements

Now you are ready to make your first plum tree drawing.

a] Start with the trunk, then the branches; the way these are placed will determine the composition (remember that a composition should highlight the beauty of blank space). Try to create an interesting pattern of branches and twigs, with some overlapping *(Fig. a)*.

b] Draw the plum blossoms. Add life to the image by introducing buds as well as half-open and fully opened blossoms. Vary their sizes and make them face in different directions.

Fig. b

Add three black points for the calyx that connects each flower to the branch. Resist the temptation to draw too many blossoms, as this will spoil the delicacy of the work. To paint plum blossoms in color, first draw outlines in black ink *(Fig. a and Fig. b)*. When they are completely dry, tip a clean brush with red ink and add a touch to each petal. These touches of red create attractive highlights.

c] To make the tree look old, add some black points here and there to suggest moss growing on the bark. As the finishing touch, add small dots at the tips of the branches to signify young, tight buds *(Fig. c)*.

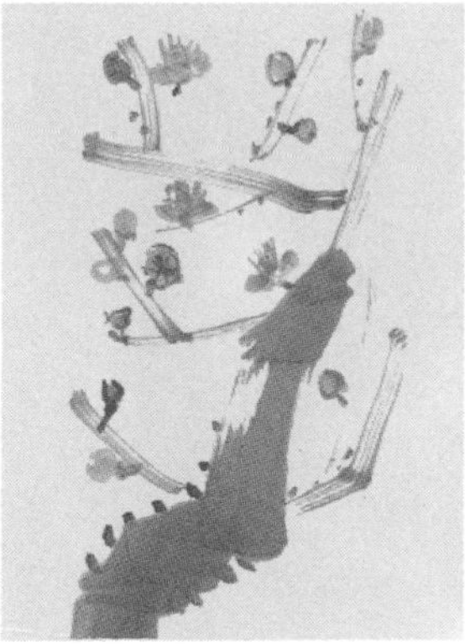

Fig. c

The Orchid

Unlike the showier varieties of orchid, the Oriental orchid is small and has tiny but beautiful, intensely fragrant flowers that bloom in spring. Because it grows in inaccessible places—forests, mountains, and clifftops—the orchid has come to represent a gentleman of purity and refinement who lives modestly.

The orchid you are going to draw in this lesson is one native to Japan, with only one small but perfect flower on the end of a stalk. The long, gracefully curving leaves make sharp, sinuous lines that contrast with the soft, oval shapes of the petals; this provides a good subject on which to learn brushwork control.

Fig. a

Fig. b

BASIC BRUSHSTROKES
Orchid Flower

a] Dip a medium-sized brush in gray ink. Squeeze out the excess, then dip the very tip of the brush in black ink. In sokuhitsu, angle the brush and draw a petal in one stroke, maintaining light pressure. The ink tone will gradually lighten from the tip to the base, accentuating the petal's curve. Try drawing petals with strokes in various directions. Draw quickly and lightly, making them look natural and lively *(Fig. a)*.

b] Put in two small solid ovals in dark ink for the heart of the orchid. The heart plays an important role in the depiction of an orchid *(Fig. b)*.

Fig. c, 1

c] Using the small-sized brush, practice drawing three or four points that look like the Chinese characters in *sosho*, a style of calligraphy *(Fig. c, 1)*. The key is to dot in the center of the flower to make it look fresh and lively *(Fig. c, 2)*.

Fig. c, 2

d] Just before the ink for the petals is completely dry, draw the center in dark ink *(Fig. d)*.

Fig. d

Fig. a

Fig. b

BASIC BRUSHSTROKES
How to draw the calyx and stem

a] Using a medium-sized brush, draw a calyx with weak ink in sokuhitsu mode from the joint connecting to the flower. Place the calyxes overlapping one another in two strokes. They should look as if they are embracing a bud or a flower *(Fig. a)*.

b] Draw a stem, preferably making it a little bit thinner and neat. The stem wrapped in calyxes and the one stretching out from the calyxes should form one straight line *(Fig. b)*.

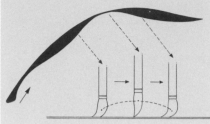

Fig. b

BASIC BRUSHSTROKES
Orchid leaves

The sword-like leaves must be smooth and sharp-edged: make sure there is not too much water in your brush, otherwise the ink will spread. Make the nearer leaves dark, those farther back light in tone.

a] Load a large or medium-sized brush with black ink, wipe off the excess, and draw the first leaf. Hold the brush upright and, starting at the base of the plant, slowly pull it upward using chokuhitsu in a long, supple, arching stroke, following the natural flow and curve of the slender leaf *(Fig. a)*.

b] To draw a twisted leaf, lift the brush gradually until only the very tip touches the paper to make the line very thin, then increase the pressure to make it thicker again. Reduce the pressure gradually as you reach the pointed tip of the leaf, lifting the brush smoothly off the paper *(Fig. b)*.

Fig. a

Sumi-e: The Art of Japanese Brush Painting

c] Practice drawing leaves in a group curving in different directions. The bases of the leaves should all start from the same point, regardless of their direction *(Fig. c)*. Envisioning the way the leaves grow in nature, draw the line from the bottom of the paper to the top in chokuhitsu mode. Make the line lithe and tense *(Fig. c, 1)*. Add pressure gradually to make the leaf thick *(Fig. c, 2)*. Lift the brush gradually to express a folded or twisted leaf *(Fig. c, 3)*. About halfway along the length of the leaf, start reducing the pressure gradually, then lift the brush quickly and smoothly *(Fig. c, 4)*.

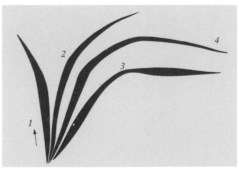

Fig. c

Combining
the elements

When you are skilled in drawing
each component, draw a whole
orchid plant. Here is an abridged
way of drawing an orchid flower.
If you want to draw your flower
with calyxes, see page 45.

a] First, draw the flower and stalk
with pale gray ink *(Fig. a)*.

b] Before the petals are completely
dry, paint the center of the flower
with black ink *(Fig. b)*.

c] Draw the leaves with black ink.
Each leaf must be drawn in one
stroke, until all the ink in the brush
is used *(Fig. c)*.

d] Add some narrower leaves
arching gracefully outward *(Fig. d)*.

Fig. a

Fig. b

Fig. c

Fig. d

The Four Gentlemen (Shi Kunshi)   [**49**]

LESSON FOUR

The Chrysanthemum

The chrysanthemum is the last of the Four Gentlemen since it is associated with the fall and its execution requires the use of all the techniques acquired in learning to paint the bamboo, the plum, and the orchid.

The chrysanthemum is a noble flower and for centuries it has been the symbol on the crest of the Japanese Imperial House. Because it is long-lasting and blooms until the late fall, it symbolizes moral strength and fortitude.

Chrysanthemums are popular garden flowers in China and Japan and come in a multitude of glorious forms and colors. In many places the air is filled with their fragrance. In this lesson, you are going to learn how to draw a kind of chrysanthemum that was very popular about two hundred years ago. Because of its simple but lovely shape, many painters of the time, Jakuchu Ito (1716–1800) in particular, favored this chrysanthemum above all others.

Sumi-e: The Art of Japanese Brush Painting

Fig. a

Fig. b

Fig. d

Fig. c

BASIC BRUSHSTROKES
Chrysanthemum flower

a] Use a small brush. Draw the first petal in two strokes, from the tip to the base *(Fig. a)*.

b] Continue petal by petal, starting at the center and building up tiers of petals to form the round shape of the flower. Keep the image of the fully blooming chrysanthemum in your mind while you are drawing the flower *(Fig. b)*.

c] When the petals are almost dry, add black points at the center of the flower *(Fig. c)*.

d] Finally, draw in the stem using dark ink *(Fig. d)*.

Fig. a

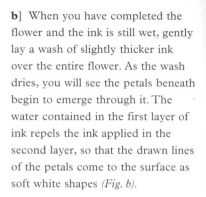

Fig. b

b] When you have completed the flower and the ink is still wet, gently lay a wash of slightly thicker ink over the entire flower. As the wash dries, you will see the petals beneath begin to emerge through it. The water contained in the first layer of ink repels the ink applied in the second layer, so that the drawn lines of the petals come to the surface as soft white shapes *(Fig. b)*.

c] Wait for the flower to dry, then draw a small circle in the center of the bloom *(Fig. c)*. Try the sujimegaki technique in red ink, too *(Fig. d)*.

Now try another technique called *sujimegaki*, which the great master Jakuchu Ito favored for his chrysanthemums. For this you will need a good-quality, absorbent paper—sized and coated papers are unsuitable for this technique. The results can be exquisite, but the shade of ink is crucial. Practice repeatedly, and you will get the hang of it.

a] Soak the brush in very weak ink—almost water—and squeeze out the excess. Draw the petals as tiny circles radiating from a central point. Try not to overlap any petals. Keep in mind the curve and shape of the whole bloom and change the curve and length of the petals accordingly *(Fig. a)*.

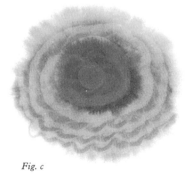

Fig. c

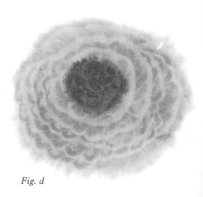

Fig. d

Fig. a

BASIC BRUSHSTROKES
Chrysanthemum leaves

a] You will need a large brush loaded with medium ink to draw the shapes of the leaves. The leaves have deep indentations, dividing them into three to five lobes. Use the body of the brush to capture the gesture of each lobe. Vary the tone of the ink and the pressure on the brush to give a feeling of movement, light, and shade to the leaves. You can draw them in sokuhitsu or chokuhitsu. When the ink has dried, use a small brush to draw the veins with darker ink. Use a rather dry brush, to make clean lines, and draw lightly. Don't attempt to draw every single vein— let the few suggest the many *(Fig. a)*.

Combining the elements

You should determine the composition as a whole before you start to draw. Where will the leaves and flowers be positioned on the paper, in which direction will they face, and how will the stalks be shaped?

a] Draw the flowers first. Vary their size and color. Make them face in different directions, and include buds, half-open blooms, and fully opened blooms *(Fig. a)*.

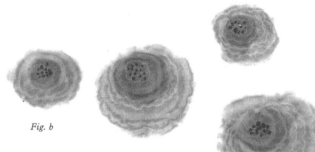

Fig. b

b] Then draw in circles in slightly thicker ink in the center of each flower. This hints at the direction in which each flower faces *(Fig. b)*.

c] Draw the leaves, making sure they do not overlap the flowers. Draw them rhythmically and observe how some are flat, curled, facing upward, or bending down *(Fig. c)*.

d] Draw the main stalk in chokuhitsu, then add the connecting stems. Draw in the veins with sharp, clear lines to reflect leaves swaying in a cool fall breeze. In a freer style, add the outlines of the leaves to complete the whole picture *(Fig. d)*.

Fig. a

Fig. c

Fig. d

PART FIVE

Increasing Your Repertoire

This section introduces some additional strokes and techniques to help you to enlarge your repertoire and make the practice of sumi-e more challenging. By adding to the basic techniques of the Four Gentlemen, you will find yourself able to tackle a wide variety of plants, flowers, vegetables, and wildlife.

Part One mentioned that sumi-e had undergone a distinctive transformation in Japan and had developed in quite different directions from the brush painting in China where it originated. Perhaps one of the principal qualities of Japanese sumi-e is the strong awareness that many works show of the changing seasons and their different moods. Seasonal differences are marked in Japan; each season has been given its own symbols in nature, and these symbols are considered excellent subjects for drawing and painting.

The following pages introduce new subjects divided into three broad categories: seasonal symbols, vegetables, and wildlife. Some drawings have been modeled on sumi-e classics from the great masters of the genre. There are two reasons for this: first, the classic works show the beautiful economy of good sumi-e painting and, second, their simplicity makes them good subjects for the beginner.

Above: Pines in the Snow, *by Maruyama Okyo (c.1780). For the Japanese, the pine tree represents the winter time and is symbolic of longevity.*

The seasonal symbols

Spring is represented by a willow tree and a dandelion plant; summer by morning-glory; fall by the rice plant and the chestnut; and winter by the pine tree. The following pages introduce these subjects.

All these symbolic plants have been popular subjects from the beginning of the sumi-e tradition, particularly with painters from the Rinpa school of the seventeenth century. Should you get the chance to study Japanese brush paintings in a gallery or museum, look for the great works of this school, by masters such as Koetsu Honami, Sotatsu Tawaraya, and the brothers Korin and Kenzan Ogata. Their paintings had a strong influence on the European art world when they were introduced to the West at the end of the nineteenth century, and they have been inspirational to many artists ever since.

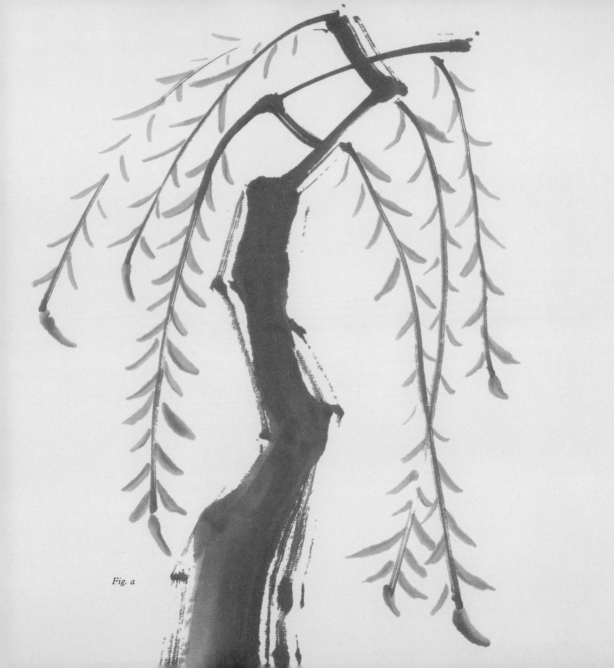
Fig. a

SPRING
The willow tree

In Japan in the springtime, as the cherry blossom falls, the willow trees start to display their greenery. The supple branches swaying in the wind resemble a waterfall, growing upward from the thick trunk. As the willow branches descend in wavelike shapes, the impression is especially graceful.

a] Draw the tree's trunk in sokuhitsu, creating its characteristic angular form. Then attach the sinuous branches, drawing each one slowly in chokuhitsu, keeping a steady, simple line from base to tip *(Fig. a)*.

b] Add the leaves, using the same technique you learned for the leaves of the bamboo but keeping your strokes a little shorter and slightly more curved *(Fig. b)*.

Fig. b

Fig. c

c] Place the leaves on alternate sides of the branches, working from the top of each branch to the end. Place a single leaf stroke at the very tip of the branch *(Fig. c)*.

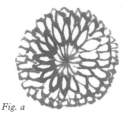

The dandelion

Spring brings dandelions to the fields of Japan. They are sometimes so numerous that they look like a dense carpet of rich green patterned with bright yellow spots. The impression they give is one of freshness and vitality, and they have long been accepted as symbols of springtime in Japanese art. Their name in Japanese means "drum flower," since the shape of two flowers entwined is similar to that of a *tsuzumi*, or Japanese drum.

a] Start with the simple round shape of the flower. Working outward from the center, form the shape of each petal with two brushstrokes, following the same sequence as you learned for drawing a chrysanthemum *(see pages 50–55)*. The flower is made from four circles of overlapping petals. Don't worry about making the circles absolutely even—the character of the flower will be created from slight variations in the size and shape of the petals *(Fig. a)*.

Fig. a

b] Make the plump, vertical stalk of the dandelion with two lines drawn in chokuhitsu, from stem to root. Try to keep them almost parallel with each other; they should be more or less the same distance apart all down their length because dandelion stems do not taper. Draw the outlines of the leaves in chokuhitsu, using the tip of the brush and working rhythmically around the shape of each leaf to form its indentations. Then draw a single vein down the center of each with smaller veins radiating off it at regular intervals *(Fig. b)*.

Fig. b

c] The background of your dandelion plant should be drawn in several horizontal lines in sokuhitsu mode *(Fig. c)*.

Fig. c

SUMMER
The morning-glory

Although some very early Japanese writings place the morning-glory in fall, the plant had become a seasonal symbol of summer by the Edo period and nowadays is considered particularly redolent of the season. It remains a popular subject for prints and paintings and is grown widely in gardens all over Japan.

a] The lightest touches of the brush will be most effective to capture the thin funnel of each morning-glory flower and its delicate calyx. Start with the "face" of the flower, drawn in sokuhitsu in four individual strokes. The petals of the morning-glory flower are not divided, so your brushstrokes should overlap in order to give the impression of the funnel's indentations. Two or three quick, light strokes in chokuhitsu will form the calyx. Smooth the tip

Fig. a

Fig. b

Fig. c

of the brush before making them, then work downward from the petals toward the stem *(Fig. a)*.

b] The leaves are worked in sokuhitsu, with two strokes forming each of the three lobes, and all the strokes worked outward, to the leaf tips. Add the veins last, working over the leaf shapes in chokuhitsu *(Fig. b)*.

c] To draw the tendrils, turn back to the practice on drawing circles *(see page 25)*, and create loose, linked circle shapes *(Fig. c)*.

FALL
The rice plant

The rice plant symbolizes a fruitful harvest to the Japanese. Here, it has been drawn in the naturalistic style of Okyo Maruyama, an artist who made his subjects look real but who also imbued them with an individual character through delicate stresses in line work and subtle variations in the tones of ink.

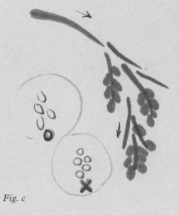

Fig. a

a] Begin by drawing the leaves and stalks, using the same technique that you used in drawing the orchid plant *(see pages 42–49)* and using mixed shades of ink. Using fast, slight lines, draw the leaves of the rice plant upward, from the root to the tip *(Fig. a).*

b] After the first process is complete, add more leaves and stalks in a slightly darker shade of ink. *(Fig. b).*

Fig. b

Fig. c

c] The ears of the rice plant are rendered with tiny dots of a darker color. They look most realistic when they are drawn in a slightly oval, rather than round, shape, with a quick, neat dab of the brush. To draw a line of rice grains quickly, angle the brush slightly to either left or right, whichever is easier for you, then work along a single stalk adding dots on either side. To give a more three-dimensional impression, vary the tone of the ink slightly as you work *(Fig. c).*

The chestnut

Chestnut trees are one of the oldest
cultivated species in Japan, and the
nuts have been part of the Japanese
diet for thousands of years.
Plantations of chestnut trees are
often found near the sites of ancient
ruins; chestnut sweetmeats are still
made today, and the branches of the
tree brought indoors to celebrate the
season. The contrasts in shape and
texture between the green, spiky
balls containing the nuts and the
smooth, glossy leaves are enjoyable
to capture in painting.

Fig. a

a] Draw the chestnut branch from base to tip in chokuhitsu, using variations in the depth of your ink. Start by drawing the whole branch in quite pale ink, then add some extra-long strokes in a medium ink, then finally a few strokes in a dark shade. The variations in shade will make your branch appear three-dimensional *(Fig. a)*.

b] Chestnut leaves are different front and back. Use two different shades to capture this, so that your leaves appear to be moving in the breeze. Draw the leaves outward from stem to tip in the paler shade, then go over the area from the stem to the "turn" of the leaf in darker ink *(Fig. b)*.

Fig. b

c] A chestnut burr is almost a full sphere. First, paint overlapping sokuhitsu strokes in weak ink to create a round shape. When it is completely dry, add short, sharp lines with the tip of the smallest brush in thick ink to represent the prickles of the burr. The ideal spikes should not look too hard: this painting is intended to show young, green burrs that will not harden and break for some time *(Fig. c)*.

Below: Work the spikes on your chestnut burr with definite little strokes. They should go in all directions to give a realistic impression of the hedgehog spikes of a real chestnut burr.

Fig. c

Fig. b

Fig. c

WINTER
The pine tree

A famous Japanese essay, penned in the fourteenth century, tells its readers: *"Grow only cherry and pine trees in your garden"*—and the pine and cherry remain indisputably the best-loved trees in Japan. A mature pine tree also represents long life and a young one, vitality, for the trees grow fast, sometimes as much as 18 inches (50 cm) in a single year.

a] The trunk and branches are drawn with the same technique as that used for the plum tree *(see pages 38–39)*, but with broader strokes. Make sure the brush is holding plenty of thick ink, then press it onto the paper and draw a thick line forcefully, going over it with additional strokes if necessary. The darker, gnarled detail on the trunk is added when the ink is almost dry *(Fig. a)*.

b] Japanese artists use a stylized form in sumi-e to represent the masses of the pine needles. First, shape an oval form with groups of three strokes. Practice using your brush at different pressures until you are making shapes that look bold and confident *(Fig. b)*.

c] Place a group just above one of the tree branches. Then add fine lines in chokuhitsu, radiating out from the trunk, to attach a group of needles to the tree *(Fig. c)*.

Fig. a

Drawing vegetables

Although you may think of them as ordinary, everyday subjects, vegetables have been depicted in many great works of sumi-e with striking naturalism and delicacy. The artist Jakuchu Ito was particularly well known for his skill in depicting them—he is said to have worked as a greengrocer as well as being a painter, which may account for his acute observations! One of his most famous works is a six-panel screen, each panel depicting a different vegetable, which he painted at the age of eighty-one, and which has a charming, almost childlike simplicity. The daikon radish and the shiitake mushroom shown on these pages were painted with this attractive, naive style in mind.

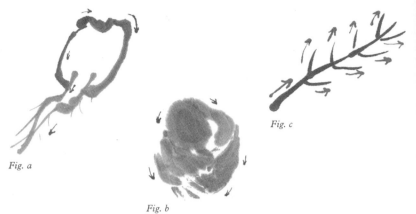

Fig. a

Fig. b

Fig. c

The daikon radish

This radish is one of the ingredients of a special rice porridge traditionally eaten on January 7 in Japan, which is believed to bring good health for the rest of the year. The radish itself symbolizes a renewal of good health and strength—in Zen art, a radish is sometimes used as a symbol of Buddha himself.

a] Start by drawing the outline of the radish root in chokuhitsu. The outline should be simple and energetic, so keep practicing until you are able to draw the root confidently and achieve a three-dimensional effect *(Fig. a)*.

b] The round-tipped, spreading leaves of the radish are drawn in sokuhitsu with varying tones of ink. Start with a full brush and do not stop drawing until the leaves are finished. The ink tone will change as you draw, resulting in a lively effect: some parts dense, others fine *(Fig. b)*.

c] When you have finished and the leaves are completely dry, add the leaf veins in chokuhitsu, using the point of the brush *(Fig. c)*.

The shiitake mushroom

The shiitake mushroom drawn by
Jakuchu Ito seems to have outgrown
the area of the page, giving an
especially striking effect. When you
are drawing the mushroom, keep
its qualities in mind: the cap is
thick and damp, and the gills
underneath are delicate and fine.
Try to capture the textures in your
finished painting.

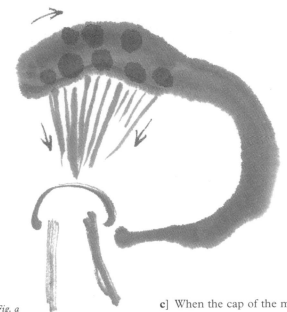

Fig. a

a] Load the brush heavily with ink,
then draw the shape of the
mushroom cap in sokuhitsu,
overlapping your strokes *(Fig. a)*.

b] Next, draw the mushroom stem
without redipping your brush, so it
appears in sparser, drier lines,
creating an interesting texture
contrast with the cap *(Fig. a)*.

c] When the cap of the mushroom
is dry, reload your brush and then
make some darker irregular spots
on it. Finally, draw the gills, working
in chokuhitsu with the point of the
brush and from the outside of the
cap toward the stem. The gills
should not overlap—as you finish
each line, lift the brush quickly
to avoid smudging one gill with
another *(Fig. a)*.

Drawing wildlife

Some of the drawings in this section have been based on the work of the seventeenth-century artist Hachidaisanjin. I discovered his work in the course of research for this book and was delighted and astonished by it. It is surprisingly abstract for its date, and he draws in an extremely simple, yet very expressive way that still seems modern today. If you draw a bird following his style from the example given on pages 80–81, you will understand the eloquence that small, individual strokes can give to the finished result.

Fig. a

Sumi-e: The Art of Japanese Brush Painting

The horse

This example is taken from the work of Korin Ogata, who created it as a design for a ceramic. The horse looks roughly drawn at first glance, but its lively posture expresses energy and movement in a very appealing way.

a] Begin by drawing the outline of the body stroke by stroke. Use the technique you learned to paint plum tree branches on page 39. Lift your brush between strokes, but maintain a smooth, sweeping motion for each stroke *(Fig. a)*.

b] Add the ears, mane, and tail quickly in sokuhitsu *(Fig. b)*.

Fig. c

The deer

The artist Sotatsu Tawaraya illustrated a scroll of the sutra "Heike Nokyo" with a deer like this.

a] Start with the head, taking care to draw the eye in a gentle curved oval, and adding antlers if you wish *(Fig. c)*.

b] Then work the body from head to tail and add the legs. A few light spots will give a dappled effect to the deer *(Fig. d)*.

Fig. b

Fig. d

The carp

This carp is a close copy of one painted by Jakuchu Ito. You see only the upper half of the fish's body as it jumps from the water. This is one of the more complex exercises in the book, so practice the different steps until you feel confident about putting them together.

a] Begin by outlining the carp's head with a pale shade of ink. Add dark strokes around the top of the head and in the center and circle of the eye for a natural effect *(Fig. a)*.

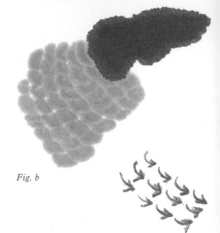

Fig. b

Fig. a

Fig. c

b] The scales should be drawn in sujimegaki, as you learned when you painted the chrysanthemum on page 52. Draw each scale in a single stroke, using a weak distillation of ink and working from the head toward the tail in waves, as shown by the arrowed brushstrokes. When the technique is effective, the scales are seen individually, without blending together too closely *(Fig. b)*.

c] Use sujimegaki again to draw the fins, in quick, separate strokes. When they are completely dry, add some fine lines with medium ink *(Fig. c)*.

The spiny lobster

Once again, the inspiration for the lobster is a drawing by Jakuchu Ito. Spiny lobsters are considered to be very auspicious, so the original work probably once hung in a rich man's house to celebrate the New Year. The artist's sea creatures (he also painted an octopus, a turtle, and squid) all have the same delicacy and lightness of touch, and in painting them he made extensive use of his favorite technique, sujimegaki.

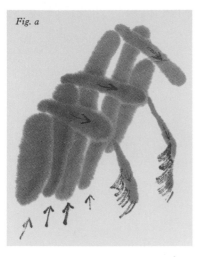

Fig. a

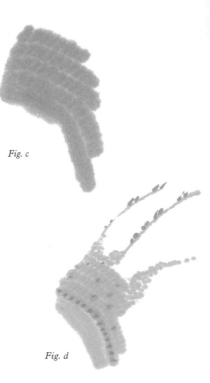

Fig. c

c] Then paint the body using sujimegaki. Use medium ink and make the strokes lightly, trying not to let them overlap as you work *(Fig. c)*.

d] When the body has dried a little, add some more short strokes with slightly darker ink *(Fig. d)*.

e] To paint the lower end of the body, closest to the tail, work a number of curved parallel lines in sokuhitsu with a darker shade of ink.

a] Start your drawing with one of the lobster's front legs with fine brushstrokes. When you have one leg placed correctly, add the others overlapping it *(Fig. a)*.

b] Outline the head with weak ink and place the round eyes with thick ink. Add dots and whiskers to the head only when it is completely dry, with a light touch of the tip of the brush *(Fig. b)*.

Fig. b

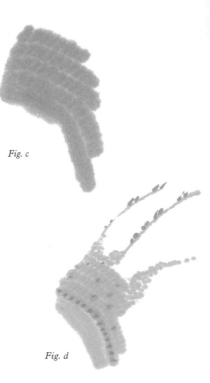

Fig. d

Birds

The examples shown here were modeled on work by Hachidaisanjin. Very little is known about this painter, but he left many examples of commissioned work, and all share the same liveliness and individuality. This is a freer style than most of the other examples, so experiment until you get a feeling for your own style.

Fig. a

a] Start by painting the eye; variations are shown in *Fig. a*.

b] Then work the head and beak around the eye with bold, confident strokes *(Fig.b)*.

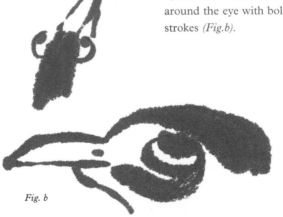

Fig. b

c] The birds' feathers are drawn freely in a mixture of sokuhitsu and chokuhitsu styles with a brush that has been heavily loaded with ink. Vary the ink tones to express the crispness and softness of the feathers' texture *(opposite)*.

Experimental Techniques

Art in Japan has evolved from centuries-old beliefs and traditions, based on a Taoist philosophy that sees the unifying pattern of life in all natural forms. Our ancestors believed that there were gods everywhere—in the sky and the ocean, in plants, trees, mountains, and rivers. These elements of nature were worshiped and loved, and the gods generously gave the people the fruits of nature at harvest time. Over the centuries, the Japanese have developed many beautiful, eloquent, yet formal expressions of their affinity with nature in their arts and crafts, including sumi-e.

Japanese artists have a common understanding of the formal conventions and symbolic meanings governing the depiction of nature, which came originally from China. For example, in a picture of a bird on a plum branch, the bird is inevitably a bush warbler. This is because the plum is a harbinger of spring and so is the bush warbler. Thus the plum is never depicted in any season but winter, when the blossom is at its best and before the leaves have begun to show in spring. Another example would be "the moon and flying wild geese." The moon is a symbol of fall and so is the wild goose; therefore, even in a picture where the birds flying across the moon are not immediately recognizable as geese, it is read that they are. While this formality and adherence to tradition is a part of Japanese culture, it does mean that painters can become trapped by mannerisms and dull conventions, which are at odds with the modern love of spontaneity and freedom of expression.

Right: Use the techniques you have learned to create your own style of sumi-e. There are many depictions of rivers in Japanese art, both ancient and modern. In this work, The River, I wanted to express the sensations of calm, happiness, and gentleness that a river evokes.

In this final section, I would like to show you some of my own sumi-e works, which express my ideas on nature's elements—the sun, moon, and stars; clouds, wind, and rain; light and dark; mountains, rivers, and waves. While they are rooted in the philosophical traditions of sumi-e, they are not drawn in the traditional style. I wanted to push back the boundaries and create new styles of sumi-e that appeal to modern sensibilities.

Having followed the lessons and learned the "language" of sumi-e, you can use it to give voice to your own thoughts and to communicate your moods, feelings, and intuitions. I hope that the drawings in this section will inspire you to try experimental techniques that will lead you in new directions and ultimately to your own personal approach to sumi-e. Be ambitious and you will find your own form of expression.

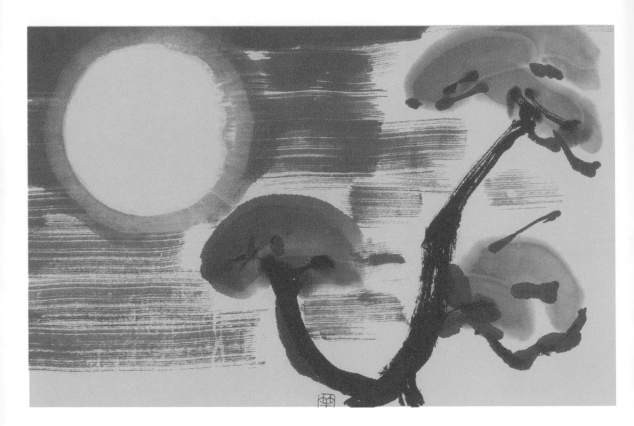

THE MOON

Living in the countryside, I like to watch the moon rising in the eastern sky over a pine forest if the night is fine. It is interesting that the moon looks very different in its color and shape depending on my state of mind. The theme here is "the moon as I see it," which is very different from the formal motif of "the moon and flying wild geese" found in traditional Japanese painting.

THE SUN

The Japanese tend to prefer the subtle lights and shadows created by moonlight to the bright light the sun sheds upon everything. Nevertheless, a motif highly popular with Japanese children is that of the sun shining over Mount Fuji. During the creation of this sun painting I felt as if I had become a child again.

THE STARS

Tanabata, the Chinese festival of stars, is celebrated each year on July 7th. Strangely, the stars as a motif have rarely appeared in Japanese art. I think this is probably because, to the Japanese, the stars are not associated with any particular season. In this painting I have created an impression of the Milky Way, making full use of the nijimi effect (blurring). Do you sense the mysterious atmosphere that the dark sky and faint starlight produce in nature?

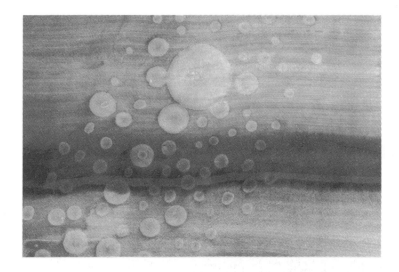

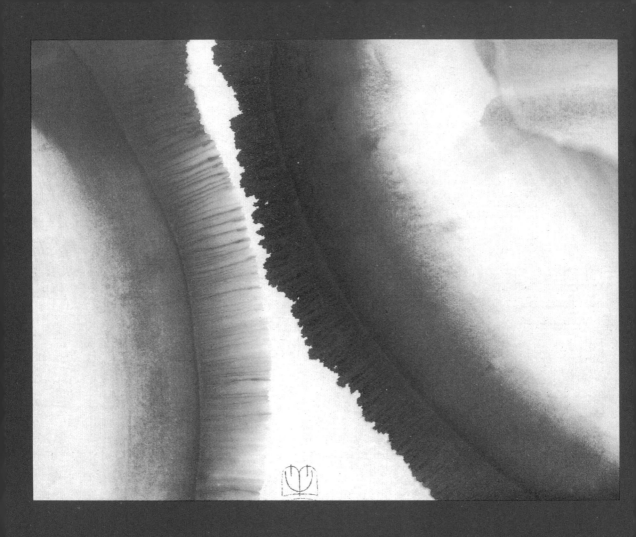

THE LIGHT

Traditional Japanese artists were not concerned with reproducing the effects of light in their paintings until Impressionism was introduced from the West in the late nineteenth century. Some innovative Oriental painters adopted Western ideas on perspective and light, but there are few examples to be found in the works of traditional schools. The color of the weak ink that I used in this work creates a wonderful effect of nijimi that feels like the dazzling diffusion of light.

THE DARKNESS

Thanks to the invention of electricity, we can enjoy long, bright nights. But thousands of years ago, nights were pitch black and made our ancestors feel afraid. Deep in the countryside, where there is no light pollution, it is possible to experience complete darkness and to imagine what it must have felt like to be huddled in a cold, dark cave, listening to the unidentifiable sounds of the night. Perhaps it would lead us to a new understanding of the world and our place in it.

Sumi, the ink, is pitch black when you make it really thick, and I have used it in this way to express my feelings about darkness in this drawing. They say that there are five colors contained in "black" ink and that you are able to sense each of them according to your state of mind.

THE RAIN

In Japan, the rainy season usually starts in the middle of June. For almost a month, it rains softly every day and night throughout the islands. It is this rain that irrigates the rice paddies that extend from the plains to halfway up the mountains. The rain, a blessing from the sky, also stimulates the young shoots on the tree branches, which we like to watch becoming denser and spreading wider day by day. The motif of clouds and rain in this picture was inspired by a pattern on a lacquer box made in the eleventh century.

THE CLOUDS

I never tire of watching the dynamic movements of clouds after rain. Sometimes, to me, the clouds seem to be living creatures with a self-contained power and a strong will. Recently I found a book of photographs taken by an American astronaut, Edgar Mitchell. He expresses clearly what I only vaguely sense when I am looking up at the fast-moving clouds in the sky. He states, in essence, that when looking at the Earth and seeing this beautiful blue and white planet floating in space, and seeing the sun in its background of velvet-black space, he knew that there was a purposefulness of flow, of energy, of time, of space in the cosmos. Suddenly it dawned on him that there was a way of understanding that was not just rational and that was beyond his previous experience.

THE MOUNTAINS

The southern slopes of the Yatsugatake range of mountains, surrounded by the Japanese Southern Alps and Mount Fuji, rise dramatically from the surrounding gentle hills with their rice paddies, fields, and villages. The mountains never fail to fascinate me, no matter how often I see them. I have tried to express this fascination through the simple, clear hieroglyph in this drawing. They say that the Chinese character for mountain was formed from the shape of a mountain, which seems to have forced its way up through the earth, trying to reach the sky.

THE WIND
The last motif, below, is the wind— one which I have been particularly interested in recently. In this work I intended to express a sensation of wide-open space, where the wind blows freely and refreshingly.

THE WAVES
The rhythmic sound and movement of waves have a hypnotic attraction. Waves depicted in Japanese sumi-e and paintings tend to be stylized and follow prescribed artistic conventions, but there are also modern works that feature realistic waves. Although the patterns used to depict the waves in this drawing are abstract, they still convey a very realistic sense of rhythm and power.

Glossary

Bokashi
Light to dark tones contained in one brushstroke.

Chokuhitsu
One of the two basic strokes of sumi-e, where the brush is held vertically and placed against the paper without leaning it sideways. This produces a thin, even stroke.

Fude
Chinese brush for drawing or writing.

Fudemaki
Bamboo mat in which brushes can be stored.

Gasenshi
Japanese handmade paper for practice.

Haboku-ho
One of the techniques to make full use of the effect of nijimi: drawing a line in weak ink at first, then adding a touch of thick ink while the first stroke is still damp.

Hissen
Washbowls for washing brushes.

Ike
A small depression at the end of the surface of an inkstone.

Kami
Paper.

Kappitsu
A dry brush technique to create a ragged line or blurred effect. After blotting the brush to remove excess water, hold the handle vertically, press it on a small plate to spread the bristles, dip the spread tip in ink, then draw a line.

Koroku-ho
Using the tip of the brush to outline shapes with thin, sharp lines.

Mokkotsu
Style of brush painting using broad strokes.

Nijimi
Soft, blurred effect created with wet ink.

Shi Kunshi
The bamboo, plum, orchid, and chrysanthemum are known as the "Four Gentlemen" (Shi Kunshi). Sumi-e beginners learn to draw these four plants, because they use all the basic sumi-e brushstrokes.

Sokuhitsu
One of the two basic strokes of sumi-e. The brush is held at around a 45° angle against the paper and leaned slightly sideways; a line is drawn using the side of the bristles. This produces a broad stroke with one sharp edge and one soft edge.

Sosho
A style of Chinese calligraphy that is characterized by very elegant and fluid lines.

Sujimegaki
The subject is drawn with very weak ink first, then a round veil of slightly thicker ink is added over it. The water contained in the first layer of ink repels the sumi contained in the second layer so that figures depicted first come to the surface in a blurry white color. One of the techniques making full use of the nijimi effect.

Sumi
Chinese ink or ink stick.

Suzuri
Chinese inkstone.

Tarashikomi
To draw using water first, then adding weak ink immediately to achieve the effect of nijimi.

Tsuketate brush
The most common brush used in sumi-e. It is made with sheep wool mixed with the hair of a horse or deer and tipped with raccoon dog hair.

Washi
A general term for Japanese handmade paper.

Xuanzhi
A type of Chinese paper that is very popular with calligraphers.

Index

Acknowledgments

I would like to thank the following for their help in making this book: Sophie Collins, Publisher at The Ivy Press in the U.K., who asked me to write this book for *sumi-e* beginners after she had seen some of my works on my Web site.

I started my career as a calligrapher and later turned my hand to *sumi-e*. Perhaps that makes my style rather unusual in comparison with ordinary, traditional styles of *sumi-e*.

With Sophie's great encouragement in the course of this project, I reaffirmed that my style would appeal to many people in the modern world. To her, I owe a special debt of gratitude.

I would also like to give special thanks to Hiromi Uchida, Editor at McDavis Associates, for running my Web site for years and to Yukiko Mima, writer, for her help with translating the text from Japanese into English and for typing the draft. Both Hiromi and Yukiko are responsible for the existence of this book.

Picture Credits

The publisher would like to thank the following for the use of pictures:

CORBIS   Burstein Collection: 57; Kimbell Art Museum: 8; Sakamoto Photo Research: 7, 10, 11.